ANIMAL ARCHITECTS
ANTS

by Karen Latchana Kenney

po_go

Ideas for Parents and Teachers

Pogo Books let children practice reading informational text while introducing them to nonfiction features such as headings, labels, sidebars, maps, and diagrams, as well as a table of contents, glossary, and index.

Carefully leveled text with a strong photo match offers early fluent readers the support they need to succeed.

Before Reading

- "Walk" through the book and point out the various nonfiction features. Ask the student what purpose each feature serves.
- Look at the glossary together. Read and discuss the words.

Read the Book

- Have the child read the book independently.
- Invite him or her to list questions that arise from reading.

After Reading

- Discuss the child's questions. Talk about how he or she might find answers to those questions.
- Prompt the child to think more. Ask: Have you ever seen an anthill or another structure made by ants? Did you see the ants building it?

Pogo Books are published by Jump!
5357 Penn Avenue South
Minneapolis, MN 55419
www.jumplibrary.com

Library of Congress Cataloging-in-Publication Data

Names: Kenney, Karen Latchana, author.
Title: Ants / by Karen Latchana Kenney.
Description: Minneapolis, MN: Jump!, Inc., [2017]
Series: Animal architects | Audience: Ages 7-10.
Identifiers: LCCN 2016048927 (print)
LCCN 2016050343 (ebook)
ISBN 9781620316917 (hardcover: alk. paper)
ISBN 9781624965685 (ebook)
Subjects: LCSH: Ants—Juvenile literature.
Classification: LCC QL568.F7 K4394 2017 (print)
LCC QL568.F7 (ebook) | DDC 595.79/6—dc23
LC record available at https://lccn.loc.gov/2016048927

Editor: Kirsten Chang
Book Designer: Michelle Sonnek
Photo Researcher: Michelle Sonnek

Photo Credits: kim7/Shutterstock, cover; andersboman/iStock, 1; sumana1/Adobe Stock, 3; 1/SuperStock, 4; Mark Moffett/Getty, 5; Andrey Pavlov/Shutterstock, 6-7; Yupa Watchanakit/Shutterstock, 8-9; FloWBo/Thinkstock, 10; Piotr Kamionka/123RF, 11; blickwinkel/Hecker/Alamy Stock Photo, 12-13; bonga1965/Shutterstock, 14-15; Christian Ziegler/SuperStock, 16-17; Fletcher & Baylis/Science Source, 18; T S Zylva/FLPA, 19; Oleksandr Grybanov/Dreamstime, 20-21; Juniors/SuperStock, 23.

Printed in the United States of America at Corporate Graphics in North Mankato, Minnesota.

TABLE OF CONTENTS

CHAPTER 1

WEAVING LEAVES

Weaver ants stand tall on a leaf and reach. Grabbing another leaf with their jaws, they pull. Like staples, they hold the leaves together. Now they can weave.

larva

An ant takes a **larva** in its mouth. The larva makes a sticky string. The ant moves the larva from leaf to leaf. Its string tightly weaves the **nest**. This will be the **colony's** new home.

antenna

thorax

abdomen

jaws

Ants are amazing **architects** and builders. Their bodies are made to help them build. The tiny ant has three main body parts: head, **thorax**, and **abdomen**. On its head are two long **antennae**. They reach, touch, and even smell.

An ant's strong jaws grab and move objects. Ants use them to bite, dig, cut, and lift. They are an ant's most important building tools.

Ants build nests for their large colonies. Some colonies are made of millions of ants. The queen lays eggs. Worker ants do the rest. They take care of the young. They hunt for food. These are the ants that build the nests.

Some ants build nests by weaving leaves together. Some dig through wood. Other ants make nests in the ground.

DID YOU KNOW?

There are more than 12,000 species of ants in the world! They can be found on every continent but Antarctica.

nest

CHAPTER 2

BIG BUILDERS

Wood ants make giant **mounds** above ground. They build these nests in the forest. Their mounds are nearly 10 feet (3 meters) around. The domes can be as tall as an adult human.

The ants stack pine needles, twigs, and grass. They open or close small holes in the mound. This keeps the nest at the perfect temperature.

A harvester ant nest is underground. Look at its entrance. The busy ants come and go. They bring up grains of sand in their jaws. They drop them off, making a sandy hill. It looks like a tiny volcano.

But what's underground? The ants dig twisting tunnels. They lead to many round **chambers**.

entrance

TAKE A LOOK!

Harvester ants build giant underground nests.
Larger chambers are at the top. Smaller chambers
are at the bottom. Tunnels connect them.

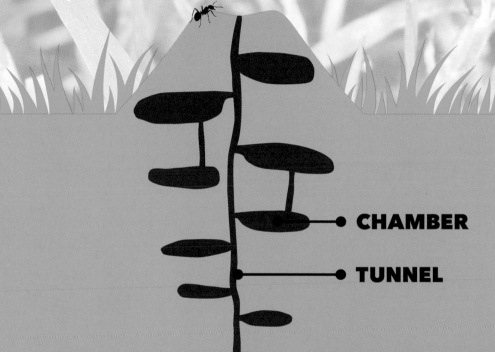

CHAMBER

TUNNEL

Ants even make nests in trees. Acrobat ants chew soil and plants. They layer papery sheets on tree twigs, branches, or trunks. They add more layers to make a rounded shape. The nest can range from the size of a tennis ball to a football.

DID YOU KNOW?

Some acrobat ants plant gardens in their nest. They put seeds on the nest. The plant roots make the nest stronger.

What if ants can't reach over a gap? Army ants build a bridge! They don't even use any materials. Their bodies become the bridge. The ants stretch across the gap. They hold on tight to each other's bodies. Then the rest of the ants march across them.

CHAPTER 3

ANTS IN NATURE

Building ants can help other animals, too. An ant nest can become a bird's home.

A woodpecker in South Asia benefits from this. It finds an acrobat ant nest. It makes a hole in the nest. Then it lays its eggs inside.

This bird usually eats ants, and the ants usually eat bird eggs. But when nesting, the bird does not attack the ants. And the ants do not touch the woodpecker's eggs.

Other ants help nature by breaking down dead trees. Carpenter ants dig their nests inside trees. **Fungus** uses the ants' tunnels. It eats the dead wood inside. This clears places in the forest for new trees to grow. It adds **nutrients** to the soil.

Ants are busy builders. Up in trees and on the ground, they work in amazing ways.

DID YOU KNOW?

Carpenter ants can damage walls inside houses. Their tunnels can make the wood weak.

ACTIVITIES & TOOLS

BUILD AN ACROBAT ANT NEST

Build a nest like the acrobat ant. Use layers of papier-mâché and see how strong it gets.

What You Need:
- tree branch
- small balloon
- tape
- newspaper
- bowl
- flour
- water
- measuring cup
- spoon

❶ **Blow up the balloon to the size of a football. Tie it and tape it to the branch.**

❷ **Mix a cup of flour with two cups of water in the bowl. Make sure there are no lumps. This is your paste. It should be runny.**

❸ **Tear the newspaper into thin strips. Dip them in the paste and lay over the balloon. Make one layer and let it dry.**

❹ **Add another layer. Let it dry. Add a few more layers. Do you feel how strong it gets?**

GLOSSARY

abdomen: The back section of an insect's body.

antennae: Two long, thin parts on an insect's head that it uses to feel things.

architects: Designers of structures.

chambers: Large rooms.

colony: A large group of insects that live together.

fungus: A type of plant that does not have leaves, flowers, or fruits, such as a mushroom.

larva: A young stage in an insect's life when it looks like a worm.

mounds: Hills or piles.

nest: A place built by animals and insects to have their young and live in.

nutrients: Substances that are essential for living things to survive and grow.

thorax: The section of an insect's body that is between its head and abdomen.

INDEX

TO LEARN MORE

Learning more is as easy as 1, 2, 3.

1) **Go to www.factsurfer.com**

2) **Enter "antarchitects" into the search box.**

3) **Click the "Surf" button to see a list of websites.**

With factsurfer, finding more information is just a click away.